ANIMAL LIVES

Mollusks
and Similar
Sea Creatures

WORLD BOOK

a Scott Fetzer company

Chicago

www.worldbookonline.com

World Book, Inc.
233 N. Michigan Avenue
Chicago, IL 60601
U.S.A.

For information about other World Book publications, visit our Web site at **http://www.worldbookonline.com** or call **1-800-WORLDBK (967-5325)**.

For information about sales to schools and libraries, call **1-800-975-3250 (United States),** or **1-800-837-5365 (Canada)**.

Editorial:
Editor in Chief: Paul A. Kobasa
Project Manager: Cassie Mayer
Writer: Daniel Kenis
Researcher: Jacqueline Jasek
*Manager, Contracts & Compliance
 (Rights & Permissions):* Loranne K. Shields
Indexer: David Pofelski

Graphics and Design:
Manager: Tom Evans
*Coordinator, Design Development
 and Production:* Brenda B. Tropinski
Book design by: Don Di Sante
Contributing Photographs Editor: Clover Morell
Senior Cartographer: John Rejba

Pre-Press and Manufacturing:
Director: Carma Fazio
Manufacturing Manager: Steven K. Hueppchen
Senior Production Manager: Jan Rossing

Picture Acknowledgments:

Front Cover: © Gérard Soury, O.S.F./Animals Animals
Back Cover: © Nikita Tiunov, Shutterstock

© Jupiter/Comstock/Alamy Images 11; © Nick Servian, Alamy Images 7; © WaterFrame/Alamy Images 28; © Bob Cranston, Animals Animals 13; © Phyllis Greenberg, Animals Animals 19; © O.S.F./Animals Animals 23; © John Pontier, Animals Animals 19; AP/Wide World 35; © Casey Dunn 37; © Nicholas Eveleigh, Getty Images 42; © Brian J. Skerry, National Geographic/Getty Images 43; © Minden Pictures 25; © Solvin Zankl, Nature Picture Library/Minden Pictures 18; © Victor R. Boswell, Jr., National Geographic Stock 17; © Bill Curtsinger, National Geographic Stock 10; © David Doubilet, National Geographic Stock 14; © Tim Laman, National Geographic Stock 5, 41; © Fred Bavendam, Minden Pictures/National Geographic Stock 21, 24; © Chris Newbert, Minden Pictures/National Geographic Stock 6; © Flip Nicklin, Minden Pictures/National Geographic Stock 32; © Birgitte Wilms, Minden Pictures/National Geographic Stock 20; © Norbert Wu, Minden Pictures/National Geographic Stock 9, 26, 27, 32; © Darlyne A. Murawski, National Geographic Stock 8, 27; © Paul Nicklen, National Geographic Stock 5; © Joel Sartore, National Geographic Stock 16; © Brian J. Skerry, National Geographic Stock 4, 29; © Maria Stenzel, National Geographic Stock 20; © Paul Sutherland, National Geographic Stock 40; © Jane Burton, Nature Picture Library 12; © Jurgen Freund, Nature Picture Library 36, 37, 38; © Matthew Maran, Nature Picture Library 22; © Duncan McEwan, Nature Picture Library 15; © Peter Scoones, Nature Picture Library 24; © Kim Taylor, Nature Picture Library 23; © Paul A. Sutherland, SeaPics.com 35; © Shutterstock 4, 8, 10, 12, 15, 17, 20, 22, 29, 30, 31, 34, 38, 39, 44, 45; © Brandon Cole, Visuals Unlimited 9; © David Fleetham, Visuals Unlimited 26, 37; © Kjell Sandved, Visuals Unlimited 40; © Rob & Ann Simpson, Visuals Unlimited 41; © Marty Snyderman, Visuals Unlimited 18; © David Wrobel, Visuals Unlimited 29.

All maps and illustrations are the exclusive property of World Book, Inc.

Library of Congress Cataloging-in-Publication Data

Mollusks and similar sea creatures.
    p. cm. -- (Animal lives)
  Includes index.
  Summary: "An introduction to marine invertebrates and their physical characteristics, life cycle, behaviors, and adaptations to various habitats. Features include diagrams, fun facts, glossary, resource list, and index"--Provided by publisher.
   ISBN 978-0-7166-0407-5
   1. Marine invertebrates--Juvenile literature. 2. Mollusks--Juvenile literature.
 I. World Book, Inc.
 QL365.363.M65 2009
 594--dc22
                    2009008853

Animal Lives
Set ISBN: 978-0-7166-0401-3

Printed in China
1 2 3 4 5 13 12 11 10 09

Table of Contents

There is a glossary of terms on page 46. Terms defined in the glossary are in type **that looks like this** on their first appearance on any spread (two facing pages).

Introduction

When you think of animals that live in the ocean, you probably think about fish. Or maybe you think about dolphins, whales, and seals. Sea turtles and sea snakes also live in the ocean.

All of these animals have something in common. They all have a backbone inside their body, just like you. But most of the animals that live underwater are **invertebrates** (*ihn VUR tuh brihts*). They have no backbone.

Snails belong to a group of invertebrates called mollusks. Mollusks have soft bodies that may be covered by a hard shell.

Ocean invertebrates

There are millions of different kinds of invertebrates. Many of these animals live in the ocean.

Ocean invertebrates come in as many shapes and sizes as you can imagine. Some look like plants, even though they are animals. Others look like gigantic insects. Some have thick, beautiful shells. Others have sharp spines on their skin. A few kinds are shaped like blobs with grasping feelers.

Invertebrate groups

Scientists group invertebrates together by the features they share. For example, **mollusks** are soft-bodied creatures that usually have an outer shell. They are the largest group of water animals. **Crustaceans** (*kruhs TAY shuhns*) are invertebrates that have a hard shell covering their entire body. Many crustaceans look like insects.

Cnidarians are a group of invertebrates that include jellyfish.

Echinoderms (*ih KY nuh durms*) are spiny-skinned sea creatures, like starfish. **Cnidarians** (*ny DAIR ee uhns*) are sea creatures that have jellylike bodies and stinging parts. Sponges look like plants, but they are a group of ocean invertebrates.

There can be many different **species** (kinds) of animals within each animal group. For example, snails and octopuses seem quite different from each other, but they are both mollusks. You will read about these animals and many other amazing sea creatures in this book.

Crustaceans, such as this crab, are invertebrates closely related to insects.

This starfish is an echinoderm, a kind of invertebrate with spiny skin.

What Are Mollusks?

If you've ever gone shelling on a beach, you've likely come across many examples of **mollusks.** The shells you collected were once home to mollusks like clams, oysters, or mussels. Like all mollusks, these animals have soft bodies with no bones. Snails, clams, squids, and octopuses are examples of mollusks.

The cuttlefish is a mollusk that is closely related to octopuses and squids. Cuttlefish are highly intelligent.

Where in the world?

Mollusks make up the largest group of underwater animals. There are nearly 100,000 **species** of mollusks, and they live almost everywhere. They can be found in lakes, rivers, oceans, and on land. Snails are mollusks that live in forests, on mountains, in the ocean, and in deserts.

Mollusk bodies

No matter where they live, all mollusks must keep their bodies moist to stay alive. Many mollusks have thick,

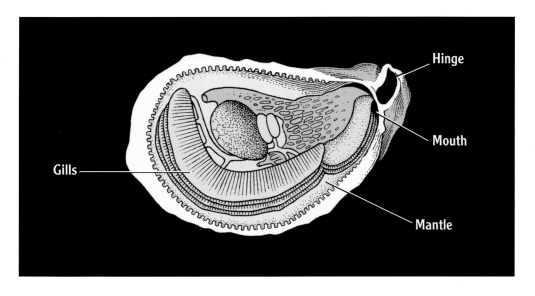

Hinge

Mouth

Gills

Mantle

Like many other mollusks, an oyster has a soft body that is protected by a shell.

hard outer shells that protect their body like a shield. Some mollusks, like squids and octopuses, do not have outer shells. But all mollusks have a skinlike covering called a **mantle.**

Some mollusk mantles have slender growths called **tentacles** attached to them. The tentacles help a mollusk sense its surroundings.

Mollusks that live in the water breathe through body parts called **gills.** Those that live on land have lunglike body parts.

The lives of mollusks

Each kind of mollusk has **adaptations** to help it survive. Squids and octopuses can zoom through the water as fast as fishes. Barnacles don't move at all, but they have tough plates that protect their bodies. Clams and other **bivalves** can clamp their shells to protect themselves.

Clams belong to a group of mollusks called **bivalves**. They live inside their shells.

Fun Fact
Mollusk shells are made from a chalklike **mineral.** Mollusks get this mineral from the food they eat. The shell grows throughout the mollusk's life.

Snails

Snails are some of the slowest creatures on Earth. They are also the most common kind of **mollusk.** The bodies of snails are usually covered with a shell. Some snails have shells shaped like tubes or cones. Other snails, like slugs, have no shell at all.

A strawberry conch is a kind of snail that lives in the ocean.

Where in the world?

Most snails live in oceans or bodies of water near oceans. They breathe with **gills.** Other snails live in rivers, lakes, or streams. A few kinds of snails live on land and breathe air with a lunglike body part.

Eyes

Tentacles

Foot

Some snails live on land. They breathe with lunglike body parts.

Snail bodies

Snails often have one or two pairs of **tentacles** on their head. One pair helps them feel their way around. The other pair often has eyes at the tip or base. A few **species** have no eyes. Instead, they use their tentacles to find their way around.

Many snails move around with a muscular body part called a foot. On land, they leave a trail of slime that helps them glide along the ground.

A snail's shell is its armor and its home. Most snails can hide in their shell. Some can even close a lidlike door over their shell opening, completely sealing themselves inside. Some land snails cover their shell openings with a door of dried slime. This helps them stay moist during dry periods.

Snail food

A snail's diet often depends on its **habitat.** A habitat is the kind of place where certain plants and animals live.

Many snails that live on land eat rotting plants. Snails that live in rivers and lakes eat plants and dead animals. Some ocean snails eat seaweed (plants that grow in water).

To eat, a snail uses a hard ribbon of small teeth to scrape and tear its food.

Sea slugs live in the ocean. Some sea slugs do not have shells.

Fun Fact

One type of snail, the sea hare, squirts out an inky liquid when it is attacked! The liquid is harmless, but it helps scare away attackers.

Bivalves

Imagine living most of your life inside a treasure chest. That is how **mollusks** called **bivalves** live their lives. There are many types of bivalves, including mussels, clams, oysters, scallops, and shipworms. Their shells are made of two valves (plates) that are connected by a hinge. The animals open and close their shells from the inside.

This giant clam is a bivalve. Its shell is made of two valves that can close tightly.

Bivalve bodies

A bivalve's body is well **adapted** for living inside a shell. Bivalves do not have heads, but they have a body part called a foot, just like snails. A bivalve uses its foot to drag itself around or to anchor itself in sand.

Bivalves have strong muscles that close their shell tight when they sense danger. Even if its shell is completely closed, a bivalve can still get food. It uses a tube near the back of its body to draw in tiny bits of food in the water through its shell. Another tube lets out waste.

Shells protect these mussels from predators. Animals have a difficult time opening them.

How bivalves use their shells

Shells protect bivalves from **predators,** who have a difficult time opening their shells. But many bivalves use their shells for more than just protection. Scallops "clap" their two shell valves together to push themselves through the water. The valves of shipworms have tiny teeth that can cut into wood. Other bivalves can attach their shells to solid rock with a cementlike substance.

Pearl makers

Some bivalve shells have treasures inside. One **species** of oyster can grow precious pearls. Pearls form when a grain of sand or dirt enters the shell, irritating the oyster's **mantle.** The oyster's body covers the grain with smooth layers of shell material to stop the irritation. Eventually, a pearl forms!

Fun Fact
You can tell how old some bivalves are by counting the rings on their shells. Each ring takes one year to grow.

A scallop uses strong muscles to try to hold its shell closed.

Octopuses and Squids

Octopuses and squids are unlike most other **mollusks.** These strange-looking animals are quite large, and they have no outer shell to protect them. But octopuses and squids make up for their lack of armor. They are the smartest and fastest of all the mollusks.

Octopus and squid bodies

Octopuses and squids have eight arms attached to dome-shaped bodies. The arms are lined with powerful suckers for grabbing **prey** (animals that are hunted). Squids also have two long **tentacles.**

Squids are usually better swimmers than octopuses. Most squids have narrow, smoothly curved bodies built for speed. But octopuses can more easily crawl around on rocks along the sea floor.

Ocean habitats

Squids live in all parts of the sea, but octopuses live in certain **habitats.** Many kinds of octopuses live close to the ocean surface. Others live in rocky, sandy, or muddy bottoms in shallow parts of the ocean. Still others live in the dark, cold waters of the deep sea.

Hunting and escaping

Octopuses and squids are skilled hunters. They eat other **invertebrates** and some kinds of fish. They

Squids are fast swimmers. Sometimes they travel in groups.

An octopus is a mollusk without a shell. Octopuses are among the smartest of all invertebrates.

Fun Fact

The biggest kinds of squids have the largest eyes of all animals. They are called the giant squid and the colossal squid. They can grow 60 feet (18 meters) long and their eyes are the size of dinner plates!

have excellent vision, which helps them catch prey.

Many animals eat octopuses and squids, including some kinds of whales, seals, and fish. Octopuses and squids squirt a dark liquid at **predators.** This liquid helps hide the animal as it escapes. Some kinds of octopuses and squids change color to blend in with their environment. An octopus can also escape danger by swimming quickly backward. If it loses an arm in an attack, it can grow a new one!

What Are Crustaceans?

Crustaceans (*kruhs TAY shuhns*) are animals that are closely related to insects. Crustaceans have a shell that fits snugly over their body like a suit of armor. A crustacean's shell is called an **exoskeleton.**

Insects of the sea

Insects and crustaceans have some features in common. They both have exoskeletons. They also have many legs with joints, like your knee or elbow. But crustaceans are different from insects. Most crustaceans live in the sea, so they have **gills** that allow them to breathe underwater.

Kinds of crustaceans

There are many kinds of crustaceans. They include lobsters, crayfish, crabs, barnacles, and shrimp. They also include tiny wood lice. Water fleas are some of the smallest crustaceans. You need a microscope to see some of them clearly! The largest crustacean is the giant spider crab of Japan. It can measure 12 feet (3.7 meters) long between its outstretched claws!

Giant spider crabs are the largest living crustaceans. Their bodies are covered in an armorlike exoskeleton.

Crustaceans and the food chain

Crustaceans play an important role in the ocean's **food chain**. A food chain is made up of plants, the animals that eat plants, bigger animals that eat those animals, and so on.

Huge numbers of crustacean **larvae** (young) float up to the surface of the ocean. There, they become part of the **plankton**. The plankton is a large group of tiny living things that blankets parts of the ocean's surface. Crustacean larvae eat the plankton. Then the larvae themselves become an important food source for fish and whales.

Wood lice are crustaceans that live in damp places on land, such as moist wood.

Crayfish are crustaceans closely related to lobsters. They are also called "crawfish."

What Are Features of Crustaceans?

A **crustacean's** body is made of sections that link together like a chain. Each of these sections is called a segment. The segments allow crustaceans to bend their bodies even though they have a hard outer shell.

A young lobster sits next to its molted shell. Crustaceans must molt, or shed, their shells as they grow.

The head

A crustacean's head includes a pair of eyes, a mouth, a pair of jaws, and three pairs of mouthparts. The mouthparts are like eating utensils. They help the animal prepare food for eating and then pass it to the mouth.

Most crustaceans have claws. This crab uses its claws for fighting and catching food.

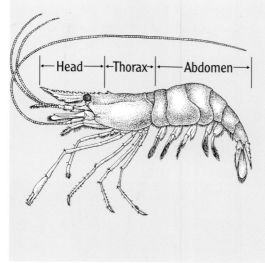

A crustacean's body has three parts: the head, the thorax, and the abdomen. Each part is made of segments.

Crustaceans also have two pairs of feelers on their head called **antennae.** They use their antennae to search for food and detect obstacles along the ocean floor.

The middle section

The middle section of a crustacean's body is called the **thorax.** It has several pairs of legs. The legs closest to the animal's head usually have claws. The animal uses these for fighting and for catching food. Crustaceans use their other legs mostly for walking or swimming.

The back end

The last group of segments makes up the **abdomen.** The abdomen may be big or small, depending on the kind of crustacean. Some crustaceans can wave the ends of their abdomen to swim backward.

Growing a new shell

As crustaceans grow, they molt (shed) their old shells and grow bigger ones. Some crustaceans stop molting when they become adults. But others molt through their entire lives.

Fun Fact

Hermit crabs are crustaceans that find empty snail shells and live inside them. Sometimes they steal the shell from snails or other hermit crabs!

Lobsters and Crabs

Lobsters and crabs are **crustaceans** known for their big claws. Their claws help them hunt for food. Their hard shells help protect them from **predators.**

Lobsters often hide out in nooks and crannies, waiting for prey to pass by.

Lobsters

Lobsters live mainly on sandy, muddy, or rocky bottom areas. Some lobsters hide in **burrows** or under rocks, waving their feelers in the water. If **prey** comes by, they dart out of their hiding spot and snatch the animal.

Lobsters have five pairs of jointed legs. The pair closest to their head is their claws. The other pairs are used for walking. Lobsters also have leglike parts on their **abdomen,** which they use mostly for swimming.

Many lobsters have one large claw with thick teeth

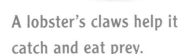

A lobster's claws help it catch and eat prey.

to crush prey and a smaller claw with sharp teeth to tear food apart. Some **species** have two big claws, and others have no claws at all.

Crabs

Crabs look quite different from lobsters. They have broad, flat bodies with a hard shell and 10 jointed legs. Their abdomen is folded underneath their body.

Many crabs have one small claw and one giant claw. They use their big claw to show how "tough" they are to other males without having to fight. But some male crabs do fight other males. They usually fight over females.

Crabs live in many different **habitats.** Some live in shallow waters. Others live in deeper waters. Some live in burrows on sandy beaches or muddy shores. A few live in fresh water or on land.

Crabs move sideways on the tips of their back legs. Some crabs have one huge claw.

Male crabs often fight each other. Sometimes they use their big claws to show how "tough" they are.

Shrimp and Krill

Shrimp and krill are **crustaceans** that look a little like tiny lobsters. They are sources of food for many animals in the ocean. Krill play an especially important role in the ocean **food chain**.

Shrimp

Shrimp live in fresh and salt water in all parts of the world. Some live near the shore, where they hide in mud or sand during the day and feed at night. Others live in the open ocean, where they feed on tiny plant- and animal-like creatures called **plankton**. Still others live in deep water, where they eat bits of food that drift down from the ocean's surface.

Shrimp come in all sizes and colors. The smallest shrimp are less than 1 inch (2.5 centimeters) long.

Shrimp live throughout the world's oceans and fresh water. This emperor shrimp clings to a sea cucumber.

Many shrimp have bright coloring, such as this Pacific striped cleaner shrimp.

A swarm of krill drifts near the ocean surface. Krill feed on tiny living things called plankton.

The largest can grow more than 1 foot (30 centimeters) long! Most are gray, brown, white, or pink, but some are red, yellow, green, or blue. Some have stripes, and some can change color to blend in with their surroundings. A few **species** can even glow in the dark!

Krill

Krill look like small shrimp floating along the surface in some parts of the ocean. They drift along with the ocean's currents and feed on plankton.

Krill are an important food source for many kinds of whales. The gigantic blue whale is the largest animal in the world. It gets all the food it needs by gulping down huge amounts of krill!

Fun Fact

A few shrimp have unusual hunting techniques. The pistol shrimp snaps its claws to shoot a powerful blast of water. This stops **prey** in its tracks!

Barnacles

Barnacles don't look like other **crustaceans.** You may have seen barnacles on the sides of ships and mistaken them for rocks. But these odd creatures are members of the crustacean family. They are the only crustaceans that stay in one place their entire adult lives.

Where in the world?

Barnacles live in oceans around the world. They can attach themselves to rocks or the hulls of ships. Sometimes, a "crust" of barnacles forms on ships that is big enough to slow them down in the water. Barnacles can even attach themselves to swimming whales!

Barnacle bodies

Barnacles have bodies that are covered with a hard, rocklike shell. Their shells are permanently stuck to hard surfaces. Barnacles also have legs that look like feelers or **tentacles.** They use them to grab bits of food drifting in the water.

Barnacles are usually small. Some are less than an inch long, but other kinds grow to about 30 inches (centimeters) long!

Barnacles can form a "crust" on different objects, including the tails of whales.

Barnacles look like rocks, but they are actually crustaceans. They stick to hard surfaces.

Barnacles get food by sticking out their feelers. The feelers grab at drifting bits of food in the water.

Young barnacles

When barnacles hatch from their eggs, they look much different from their adult form. Tiny barnacle **larvae** drift through the ocean until they take on a bean shape and grow a shell. Then they move out of the water and cling onto a solid object, where they will stay for the rest of their lives. As they grow, they form hard, fixed plates around their body.

What Are Echinoderms?

Many odd-looking sea creatures roam the sea floor. Some have spikes growing from their bodies. Others look like plants. Many of these creatures belong to a group of spiny-skinned animals called **echinoderms** (*ih KY nuh durms*). Starfish, sand dollars, sea urchins, and sea cucumbers are just a few members of this group.

Echinoderm bodies

Many echinoderms are shaped like stars or wheels with a mouth at the center. They use structures called tube feet to move along the sea floor. Each tube foot has a suction cup on the end of it. This helps the animal hold onto hard surfaces. Echinoderms also use their tube feet for breathing, eating, and getting a feel for their surroundings.

Echinoderms, such as this sea cucumber, have spiny skin. They usually live on the sea floor.

Starfish and other echinoderms use their tube feet to move and to grab prey.

Echinoderms have a bony skeleton inside their body. Spines from this skeleton often poke out through their skin. This gives many echinoderms a spiky appearance. Others look smooth because their spines are buried in their skin.

Sea lilies are echinoderms that look like plants.

Life cycle

Like many other sea creatures, echinoderms hatch from an egg. But their **larvae** look much different from adult echinoderms. They have a right side and a left side, like most other animals. And they can swim freely. When the larvae grow up, they sink to the bottom of the sea and take on a round or star shape.

Fun Fact
Even though they have skeletons inside them, echinoderms are not vertebrates. This is because they do not have a backbone.

Starfish and Sea Urchins

It is hard to imagine what starfish and sea urchins have in common with each other. One animal is star-shaped and has many arms. The other looks like a spiky ball. But these ocean animals are more alike than you may think. They both belong to the **echinoderm** family.

Starfish

Starfish are sea animals with spiny skins and thick arms. Most starfish have five arms that spread out from the center of their body. Starfish also have tube feet on the underside of their body. They use these to move along the sea floor and to pry open the shells of mussels and clams.

Starfish eat many ocean **invertebrates.** Some have an unusual way of hunting and killing **prey.** First, the starfish covers an animal with its arms. Then the starfish turns its stomach inside out and pushes it outside of its body. The stomach digests the animal and then returns to the starfish's body!

The long spines of a sea urchin protect the animal from predators.

Starfish are fierce hunters. In this photograph, a group of starfish attacks and eats sea urchins.

Sea urchins

Sea urchins are round sea animals covered with long spines. The spines are all part of the sea urchin's skeleton. Sea urchins can move these spines to wobble along the sea floor.

Sea urchins have a mouth and tube feet on their underside, just like starfish. Some sea urchins use their tube feet to cover themselves with broken bits of shell and seaweed. This helps them hide from **predators** like crabs, fish, and sea otters.

Sea urchins eat mostly plants and **algae.** They use their sharp teeth to chop down kelp, a kind of seaweed that looks like underwater trees.

A sea urchin's inner skeleton has five sections, just like many other echinoderms.

Fun Fact

If an animal eats a starfish's leg, the starfish can grow a new one. A starfish can be cut into several pieces and still live, as long as it keeps part of its center.

Sea Cucumbers and Sand Dollars

Not all **echinoderms** look bumpy or spiky. Sea cucumbers often have smooth, cylinder-shaped bodies. Sand dollars look like flat, furry disks. But like starfish and sea urchins, these animals have a skeleton inside their bodies.

A sea cucumber's spines are buried deep inside its skin.

Sea cucumbers

Sea cucumbers live along rocky shorelines, shallow seas, and the deep ocean. Their long, fleshy bodies look smooth because their spines are buried deep inside their skin.

Sea cucumbers have a mouth at one end of their body. The mouth is surrounded by **tentacles** that grab bits of food floating in the water.

Sea cucumbers also have tube feet, just like starfish and sea urchins. These help the animal crawl along the ocean floor or attach themselves to things.

A sea cucumber grabs bits of food with its tentacles. Then it puts the food in its mouth.

Sand dollars

Sand dollars often live in shallow coastal waters and spend much of their time buried in sand. They are less spiky than other echinoderms, but their bodies are covered in a fuzzy brown outer layer.

Sand dollars have many tiny, movable spines that they use to dig, crawl, and eat. The bodies of many sand dollars also have slots or notches. These help the animal draw up sand through their bodies. In this way, sand dollars can bury themselves and avoid getting eaten.

Fun Fact
Sea cucumbers have an unusual way of defending themselves. They can throw out internal body parts to distract attackers! Then they regrow new body parts.

A sand dollar's dried skeleton looks similar to old dollar coins.

Sand dollars are less spiky and more fuzzy than other echinoderms. They can bury themselves in rocks or sand.

What Are Cnidarians?

Many **invertebrates** of the sea are soft-bodied animals. They include jellyfish, corals, and sea anemones, among others. Together, they make up a group of animals called **cnidarians** (*ny DAIR ee uhns*). Cnidarians include some of the most strange-looking of all sea creatures.

Some cnidarians, such as these sea anemones, barely look like animals. They capture food with stinging tentacles.

Cnidarian bodies

One reason cnidarians may seem strange is because they are not two-sided like most familiar animals. The bodies of insects, fish, frogs, lizards, birds, cats, and human beings all have a "right side" and a "left side." So do the bodies of **crustaceans** and **mollusks.**

But cnidarians are different. Their bodies do not usually have any "sides" or "ends" at all, except for a mouth. Cnidarians may be shaped like blobs, mushrooms, worms, or even flowering plants— with waving **tentacles** instead of branches.

Fun Fact

Sea anemones are colorful cnidarians. They are named after the anemone, a kind of flower.

Jellyfish are free-swimming cnidarians. Many jellyfish have see-through bodies.

The lives of cnidarians

Each kind of cnidarian has a different way of life. Some can swim freely. Others are attached to the sea floor. Some have bodies that are almost completely see-through, like living glass. Others look like flowers. Still others grow together in large groups.

One thing all cnidarians have in common is their weapons. Cnidarians have tiny, stinging parts that they use to capture **prey.**

Corals

Some kinds of **cnidarians** can build huge structures that are like underwater cities where many different animals live. These structures are called coral reefs. They are one of the most beautiful of all ocean **habitats.** The animals that build the reefs are called corals.

Coral polyps

Corals are tiny, soft-bodied creatures that look a little like flowering plants. Each individual coral is called a **polyp** (*POL ihp*). Most polyps are less than an inch (2.5 centimeters) across. Polyps stay rooted to the ground and grab bits of food with their stinging **tentacles.**

Coral colonies

Even though a coral reef is made up of many polyps, it can also be thought of as a single, large body. This is because the corals form connected **colonies.** A colony is group of individual polyps joined together. Coral colonies are constantly growing.

Building the reef

Many kinds of corals build reefs. They do so by taking **minerals** from seawater and shedding them around the bottom of their bodies. This forms a limestone "skeleton." Over time, the limestone builds up and creates the structure of the reef. Meanwhile, older

The living animals in coral reefs are called polyps. They build the reefs by shedding minerals around their bodies.

Coral reefs form important habitats for many underwater animals. Cnidarians build the reef structure.

The Great Barrier Reef stretches along Australia's eastern coast.

corals form growths, called buds. Eventually, the buds detach from their bodies and become new corals. The new corals then attach to the top of the reef and continue the process.

The Great Barrier Reef

Coral reefs can be huge. The Great Barrier Reef along the coast of Australia is the world's largest system of coral reefs. It is made up of more than 2,000 individual coral reefs that stretch across about 1,240 miles (2,000 kilometers) of ocean.

North Pacific Ocean

Equator

Indonesia

Papua New Guinea

East Timor

GREAT BARRIER REEF

Australia

South Pacific Ocean

Indian Ocean

Jellyfish

Jellyfish are soft-bodied animals that live in all parts of the ocean. Despite their name, they are not fish at all. They are **cnidarians.** Some jellyfish live near sunny surface waters. Others live in the deep ocean.

Jellyfish bodies

Jellyfish bodies are shaped like bells. A tube with a mouth usually hangs down from the middle. Many stinging **tentacles** also hang down from the body's edges. Some jellyfish tentacles are more than 100 feet (30 meters) long!

Jellyfish bodies hold their shape because they are filled with a jellylike material. This is also why jellyfish can survive in the deep ocean. The water's pressure in the deep ocean is so great that most animals would get crushed. A jellyfish's squishy filling is like a cushion that protects the animal from the crushing pressure.

Getting around

A jellyfish swims by opening and shutting its body like an umbrella. This squeezes out water and causes the animal to shoot upwards. When it stops moving, the jellyfish starts to sink. On the way down, the jellyfish catches small animals with its tentacles. It stings them and then swallows them.

Jellyfish swim by opening and shutting their bodies like umbrellas, shooting up through the water.

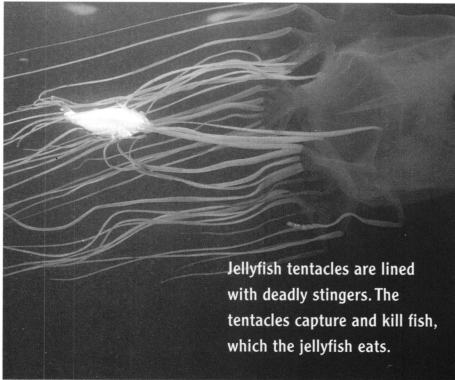

A giant jellyfish can weigh 330 pounds (150 kilograms). Its many long tentacles help it capture food.

Jellyfish tentacles are lined with deadly stingers. The tentacles capture and kill fish, which the jellyfish eats.

Fun Fact

Sea wasps are jellyfish that have a very poisonous sting. The sting of the sea wasp can kill a person in minutes. Sea wasps live along the coasts of Australia.

Portuguese Men-of-War

In warm oceans throughout the world, a strange, soft-bodied animal drifts along with the ocean's currents. It looks a little like a giant brain floating on the surface of the ocean, and it is often mistaken for a jellyfish. This animal is the Portuguese man-of-war. It has a fierce sting that can kill people.

Men-of-war bodies

The man-of-war has a clear, balloonlike float at the top of its body. This float is filled with gas. It keeps the animal on the ocean's surface and acts like a ship's sail. The float catches wind, causing the animal to drift around the ocean.

Groups of **tentacles** dangle from the float. They sting, grab, and eat animals below the water's surface.

A colony of animals

Perhaps the strangest thing about the man-of-war is that it is not a single animal. It is a **colony.** The colony is made up of individual animals called **polyps.**

Each polyp plays a special part in keeping the colony alive. Some polyps are in charge of stinging and catching **prey.** Other polyps digest the prey and share the food with the others. The big, gas-filled float on top of the man-of-war is actually a single, large polyp. In a way, the animals that make up a man-of-war colony are like the individual cells that make up your body.

The Portuguese man-of-war looks like a big jellyfish, but it is actually a colony of smaller **cnidarians.**

Individual animals called polyps make up the tentacles of a Portuguese man-of-war.

Fun Fact

Other kinds of colonies live deep below the ocean. Some of them are shaped like gigantic snakes or ribbons. These colonies contain polyps and swimming, bell-shaped jellyfish. The jellyfish pull the rest of the colony around.

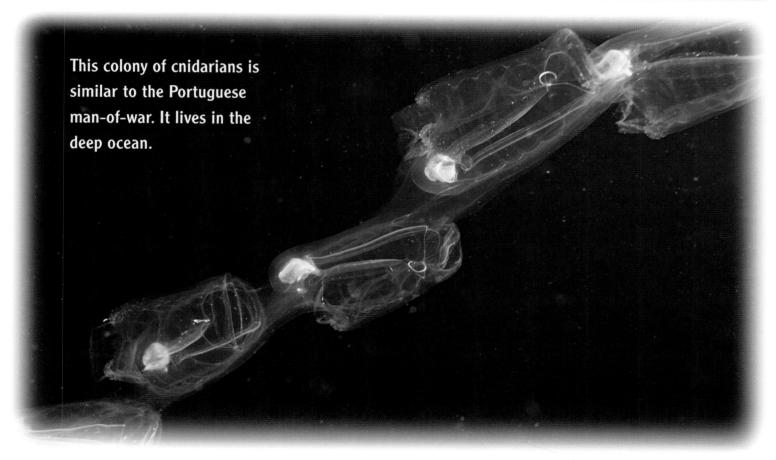

This colony of cnidarians is similar to the Portuguese man-of-war. It lives in the deep ocean.

What Are Sponges?

You may not think that sponges are animals. They don't look or act like most animals. They can look like vases or like crusts on rocks. And they never move. People once believed that sponges were plants. But today, scientists know that sponges are animals.

Ancient sea creatures

Sponges have lived in the ocean for more than 500 million years. They belong to an animal group all their own. Even though they look like plants, they share the same traits as other animals. Sponges eat their food, just like all animals. Plants can make their own food from the sun.

Sponge bodies

Sponges come in many different shapes. Some are round or shaped like a vase. Others form a crust on top of objects like rocks.

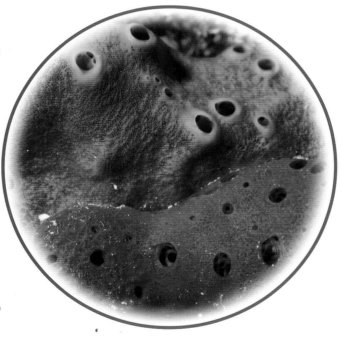

Sponges draw water into their bodies through holes. They filter and eat tiny living things in the water.

Sponges can also be many different colors and sizes. Some are less than 1 inch (2.5 centimeters) across. Others are more than 4 feet (1.2 meters) long!

Sponges look soft, but they have a skeleton that protects and supports their body. The skeleton is made up of tiny, needlelike structures. These protect the sponge from animals that try to eat it.

Sponge bodies have openings and holes. Some holes let in water and the tiny plants and animals that sponges feed on. Other openings let out water and wastes.

Sponge survivors

Like starfish, sponges are able to regrow lost or injured parts of the body. This helps sponges survive even if most of their body is eaten by an animal. You can even push a sponge through a fine mesh screen, and all the pieces would come back together!

Sponges come in many forms. They include the red finger sponge *(far left)* and the brown tube sponges shown here.

A barrel sponge pumps water up and out of the huge opening on top of its body.

How Are Ocean Invertebrates Endangered?

Underwater **invertebrates** are some of the most amazing animals on Earth. They are also among the most numerous. And yet many of them are threatened by human activities.

Huge fishing nets can drag along the seafloor, destroying invertebrate habitats.

Pollution

Pollution caused by human activities has poisoned the waters where many sea animals live. Pollution includes garbage, chemicals, and other human-made wastes. These wastes can destroy ocean **habitats**.

Garbage, chemicals, and other forms of pollution threaten animals that live in the ocean.

Coral bleaching is caused by algae leaving the bodies of coral **polyps.** The polyps depend on algae to survive.

Global warming

Invertebrates are also threatened by **global warming.** Global warming is the slow warming of Earth's surface.

One kind of animal threatened by global warming is the coral. Corals depend on **algae** in their body to get energy from the sunlight. When waters around coral reefs get too warm, the algae leave the bodies of corals, causing the animals to die.

Invaders

Some ocean invertebrates are threatened by animals that are introduced to their habitat. For example, zebra mussels compete with freshwater clams in North America for space and food, pushing them out of their habitats. The zebra mussels never bothered the clams before because they used to live far away, in Asia. Human beings brought the zebra mussels to North America on ships, and now they have become a serious pest.

Zebra mussels have become a serious pest in North America's lakes and rivers.

Protecting Ocean Invertebrates

Human activities can threaten underwater **invertebrates** in many ways. But people can also help protect these creatures. Laws and treaties (agreements between countries) can make it illegal to hunt **endangered** sea animals. Organizations can raise money to protect ocean **habitats** and educate people about the animals that live there. Each of us can do our part to help.

Learning about underwater invertebrates, and raising awareness about them, can help protect these animals.

Making laws

One way to help ocean invertebrates is to make laws that protect them. For example, the United States has created laws that forbid the hunting of endangered **species,** such as freshwater clams. Australia has created laws to protect the Great Barrier Reef from human activities that can harm it.

Taking action

People can also help many sea creatures by trying to reduce **pollution** and the effects of **global warming.** Many human activities

Scientists study how global warming affects corals. Global warming is caused by many human activities.

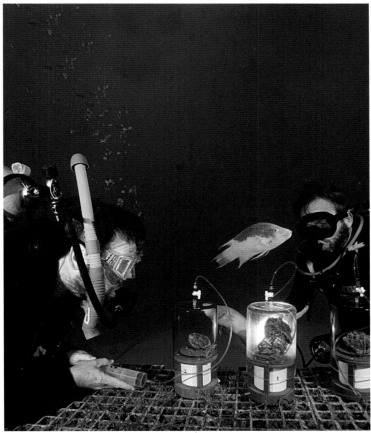

cause global warming, such as burning certain kinds of fuel to power our cars, homes, and other buildings. People can try to reduce these activities and develop cleaner sources of power.

Speaking out

Another way to help ocean invertebrates is to raise awareness about them and the threats to their environments. People might not know about some of the strange-looking creatures in our oceans and their importance to ocean habitats. By protecting ocean invertebrates, we can help keep our oceans healthy.

Activities

Name That Sea Creature!

Test your knowledge of ocean **invertebrates** by taking this quiz! You can check your answers against the answer key on this page. **Be sure to use a separate piece of paper to write down your answers.**

1. This sea creature can often be found crawling on rocks along the sea floor. If it loses one of its arms in an attack, it can grow a new one.

   a. lobster   c. octopus
   b. squid   d. jellyfish

2. This sea creature can turn its stomach inside out to feed on other animals.

   a. squid   c. oyster
   b. snail   d. starfish

3. Animals in this group of ocean invertebrates are closely related to insects.

   a. cnidarian   c. echinoderm
   b. crustacean   d. mollusk

4. This animal looks like a shrimp. It lives in large groups on the surface of the ocean. It provides food for whales and large fish.

   a. starfish   c. Portuguese man-of-war
   b. barnacle   d. krill

5. People used to think that this kind of ocean invertebrate was a plant, but it's really an animal.

   a. sponge   c. jellyfish
   b. bivalve   d. sea cucumber

6. This sea creature often lives in the deep ocean. It can survive there because its body is filled with a jellylike material.
   a. krill   c. sea cucumber
   b. jellyfish   d. sea urchin

Answers: 1: c; 2: d; 3: b; 4: d; 5: a; 6: b

Endangered Sea Creatures Research Project

Introduction: Many kinds of sea creatures are **endangered** because of human activities or other causes. The best way to protect endangered animals is to tell other people about the threats to these animals. You can find out more about endangered ocean invertebrates near your region or country by looking up information in your school or public library.

Materials:

- Poster board
- Markers

Directions:

1. Ask a family member, teacher, or your school or public librarian to help you find information on endangered ocean invertebrates near your region or country.

2. Choose an animal that you wish to learn more about. Write down important information about the animal and why it is endangered. Questions you may wish to answer include:

   - Where does this animal live?

   - What is unique about the animal?

   - What is the animal's natural **habitat?**

   - What are the main threats to this animal?

   - How long has the animal been endangered?

   - What are people doing to help protect the animal?

3. Draw a picture of the animal on the poster board. Write down information about the animal that you'd like to share with others. You can present your findings to your class, family, or friends.

Staghorn coral is critically endangered. It grows in the Florida Keys, the Bahamas, the Caribbean islands, and Venezuela.

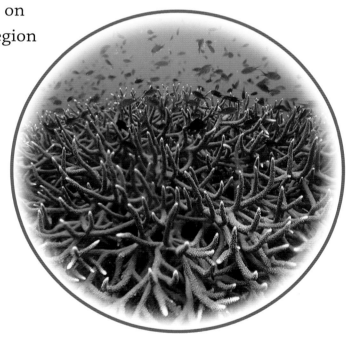

Glossary

abdomen the rear part of the body on insects and crustaceans.

adaptation; adapted a feature or trait that helps a living thing survive in its environment; fitted.

algae a group of simple, plantlike living things.

antennae long feelers that stick out from the heads of some animals.

bivalve a kind of mollusk that forms a hinged, two-part shell.

burrow a hole dug in the ground by an animal for shelter.

colony a group of animals or plants of the same kind, living or growing together.

cnidarian a type of soft-bodied water animal that has stinging tentacles.

crustacean a type of underwater animal closely related to insects.

echinoderm a type of underwater animal with a spiny skeleton.

endangered in danger of dying off completely.

exoskeleton an armorlike shell covering insects and crustaceans.

food chain a system linking animals, the things they eat, and the things that eat them.

gill the body part that a fish, tadpole, crab, or other water animal uses to breathe in water.

global warming the gradual warming of Earth's surface.

habitat a place where a plant or animal lives in the wild.

invertebrate an animal with no backbone.

larva; larvae a young version of an animal; more than one larva.

mantle a skinlike covering on animals called mollusks.

mineral a solid material found on Earth.

mollusk a type of animal with a soft body that is often covered by a hard shell.

plankton a large group of tiny organisms that live at the ocean's surface.

pollution all the ways that human activity harms nature.

polyp a wormlike water animal.

predator a hunting animal.

prey any animal or animals hunted for food by another animal.

species a group of animals or plants that have certain permanent characteristics in common and are able to breed with one another.

tentacle a long, slender, flexible growth on an animal.

thorax the middle part of the bodies of insects and crustaceans.

Find Out More

Books

Animal Kingdom Classification by Daniel Gilpin and Steve Parker (Compass Point Books, 2005-2006) 14 volumes

Five volumes in the set cover the invertebrates: **Sponges, Jellyfish and Other Simple Animals; Lobsters, Crabs and Other Crustaceans; Snails, Shellfish and Other Mollusks; Nematodes, Leeches and Other Worms**; and **Starfish, Urchins and Other Echinoderms.**

Grzimek's Student Animal Life Resource: Crustaceans, Mollusks, and Segmented Worms by Arthur V. Evans and others (UXL, 2005)

In a single volume, you'll find information on everything you ever want to know about many of the lower forms of animals. Species are arranged and described according to their classification, and are further indexed according to their habitats and their geographic location.

Sea Sponges by Deborah Coldiron (ABDO Publishing, 2008)

This book, with both basic and unusual facts about sponges, would be helpful in writing school reports.

Web sites

Biology for Kids: Invertebrates
http://www.biology4kids.com/files/invert_main.html

Learn what an invertebrate is, then link into other pages that describe different groupings of invertebrates, for example, sponges, anemones, worms, insects, and spiders.

Invertebrates
http://nationalzoo.si.edu/Animals/Invertebrates/

The Smithsonian Institution's National Zoo discusses ways people are getting involved in invertebrate study, for example, the zoo's invertebrate-collecting trip, its project to grow new creatures for a coral reef, and its special invertebrate exhibit.

Marine Invertebrates
http://www.stemnet.nf.ca/CITE/marinver.htm

A teacher at Gander Academy, an elementary school in Newfoundland, Canada, lists links to Web sites about jellyfish, barnacles, shrimp, sea worms, mollusks, bryzoa, and other invertebrates that live in the ocean.

U.S. Fish & Wildlife Service: Kids' Corner
http://www.fws.gov/endangered/kids/

The focus is on how you can get involved in saving our wildlife and conserving their natural habitats.

Index